Mike Corrao & Evan Isoline

Cephalonegativity

On the Theater of Decapitation

Cephalonegativity
On the Theater of Decapitation

Mike Corrao is a multimedia artist and the author of six books including *Smut-Maker* (Inside the Castle) and *Gut Text* (11:11 Press).

Evan Isoline is a writer and visual artist living on the Oregon coast. He is the author of *Philosophy of the Sky* (11:11 Press).

Copyright © 2021 Mike Corrao, Evan Isoline
All rights reserved

This book may not be reproduced in whole or in part, except for the inclusion of brief quotations in a review, without permission in writing from the author or publisher. No part of this publication may be reproduced, stored in or introduced into retrieval system, or transmitted, in any form, or by any means (electronic, mechanical, photocopying, recording, or otherwise), without prior permission of the publisher.

Paperback: 978-1-954899-03-2

Printed in the United States of America

FIRST AMERICAN EDITION

9 8 7 6 5 4 3 2 1

Cephalonegativity
On the Theater of Decap͟͟͟͟itation

ACT ONE

M IS PRESENT / THE STAGE IS PRESENT / THE SCENE IS PRESENT

WE ARE SPEAKING/ A PERFORMANCE OCCURS / A LAMENTATION / A LEVITATION

M (alive): O! Fat of Sow. O! Isola over ocean. O! Garb under pit. I want to drink of the surface'd fountain. Lapping slime and blood from the open reservoir. I run my life in arson percent. Burning all timber / kindling all red. Clipping under the tile floor—void access—surface is not territory (Metahaven). I wash my body over the smooth cleanness of the polymer. I think to myself *this is the fable'd ext*. With corridors that do not shut, that retreat inward, not so much inside as canopy'd by the roof of your mouth. My flesh cannot be separate'd between contain'd and container. It is all one. The piss of all suns. I want to drink from the lift'd fountain of death. Recoiling at the bitter taste of an unseason'd garnish. Wearing ugly garb as I speak into the microbial pores of the surface. Letting my wet breath flood each groove. Letting my acid breath pockmark the landscape. I stretch my hand over the horizon and think to myself, *the landscape is not a surface. The surface is not a territory. The landscape is a territory which projects the signifiers of a surface. It is a gaian microlith.* Our eyes sever once again. Information is not material. The surface can embody whatever language it desires. The platinum card is not made from platinum. The fat of the sow is not cut from the underbelly. The garb is not spawn'd from the pit. It is bunch'd in the sweating alcoves of the body.

M UNFURLS A TAPESTRY OF LINENS FROM THEIR PIT / THE TAPESTRY IS DAMP AND DISCOLOR'D / IT DEPICTS A SCENE

THE SCENE IS BURNING

Innard: *What do you wish to gain? What do you wish to create?*

**THE SCENE IS BURNING /
THE SURFACE ENGULFS THE SCENE AND SUFFOCATES THE FIRE /THE SUN IS WHINING**

M (alive): The surface emits holy evocations. The muses lifting song from my mouth. Nearly to my suffocation. Furies weeping with inconsolable familiarity. The surface is an interface. Glassy eyes drawing my hands and face. I am pressing my forehead against the surface. And it is screaming. And I am trying to shatter soft polymer with the strength of my desires. Bright fire quivering over an inflammable body. We drink from the fountain of blood. We drink from the fountain of slime. I am grafting the skin of my forearm onto the surface, hoping that its pores will take my own, that we will be unify'd once again. I feel a primordial connection between us. My anatomy is a haphazard module sever'd from its foundation. The orate'd chorus of my limbic system, of my nervous system, of the innard. I awake every night at the same time. Erect'd under the sweat of my sheets by the image of a cephalophore. My sever'd head in their hands, march'd from the body to a soft polymer altar. Graft'd onto the surface. The surface is not a territory. It is the interface. Intrafacial materials sinking into undecayable holiness. The polymer speaks the word of god. The sun fusing our bodies. I watch as it drowns my vision in eternal light, and suddenly, darkness.

DRONE EMISSIONS / SONIC DELIGHTS / SOUND CORPOREALIZES IN THE OPEN AETHER / THE MUSIC IS HEAVENLY

/ THE INSTRUMENTS ARE UNKNOWN

M (x): It is not difficult to access the void. In death or in life. There is always pitch crawling down the curve of the forehead. It can be wipe'd away, yes. But left unattend'd, it will stain the eyes black and flood the mouth. This is not death. It is only temporary. Death is not death. It is only temporary. The necromancer will revive me once again. My sever'd head emitting drone signals from its new altar'd body.

CEPHALOPHORIA / HEAD EXITS BODY DRINKING FROM A GOBLET OF BLOOD / A VAMPIRE / A LAMPREY

Head (sever'd): I inhale the sludge of god. Opening my mouth. Letting a sky of blood reign unto me. Until it has condense'd into a quivering gelatin. And I am entrance'd by its flowing body. Thinking, *I do not want to know where this blood came from. If it was always mine, or if it has pass'd through another on its way to me,* as I submerge my un-gill'd complexion. Hoping that it will emit some kind of holy aura. I am yet to discover of what nature. If it is ecological or hadean, arcadian. When the blood'd gelatin crawls into my mouth, I am no longer able to speak or breathe. I am turning purple or blue inside of this confine'd darkness.

**THE HEAD IS NOT THE BODY /
THE NECK IS THE THRESHOLD
/ THE BODY IS SEPARATE'D BY THE THIN PLANE
OF THE SURFACE**

M (sever'd): Is this the ideal means by which we might access the unconscious? Is it in the valley of deprivation? The valley of openness? I cannot see where I am going and thus my journey is unbound to the deception of the senses. I cannot be led astray by covetous images. The blood purifies my mind. It purifies my eyes and mouth.

CUT TO / INT. / A PERFORMANCE OCCURS / LEGS WRITHING AND RECOILING

**THE SCENE IS BURNING
THE SURFACE IS SOFTEN'D BY HEAT**

M (sever'd): I see through the entirety of my body. With a sense that I cannot quite describe. Something both sonic and haptic. Televisual. Static. *Navigation is something felt, not seen.* I follow the psionic pathways map'd out inside my veins. Into a desert of festering neurologies. Where there is no air left to breath. And no flesh left unprune'd.

**PITCH-BECOMING-BLOOD /
EVOKING ELEGANCE AND FREEDOM / TRANS-MUTATION
BODY GRAFT'D UNTO WOUND**

ACT TWO

The STAGE, the SCENE, where Body is in multiple points of view simultaneously, Body is not in one state, but many, headless, in *ecstasis*, standing apart, standing outside the act of thought, of pain, of desire for feeling. Away from the Head. The Head is an island, a satellite orbiting the Body.

The Head sits. The Head is a fusiform wax, glistering under the sun's livid gleam. Cochlear briquettes spit smoke from laterally oriented puckers. Head's eyes stare but with fixed intent as through a meshy expanse of darkness. The mouth avows to an *Alleluia* of pleasure, in a catabolized state. Blinded by the glare, I feel for the mouth in the Head, hooking two of my fingers along the dusky labia of the cavity into a broken smile. The mouth of the Head, the VELVET-EATER. A smashed amethyst cluster, a feline throat and mouth-roof, terraced of pink and grey palatine cross-ridges between the snaggy teeth-rows. Muculent saliva runs clear to opaline, solidifying in the recesses of the livid pocket and at the corners of the lips as a dense tallowy foam.

SCENE of the Head sitting stowed against pyrite blue sea walls. SCENE sagging against cephalesque mica suturing between ribs. Adhesion plates that stick against teeth marks on headless neck transection fattened with soft geode sand. Nothing excluded from SCENE—except the primordial applause preceding it. In a series of small expressions, the Head (its voice is all over the stage) reaches the exclamation point, and for all bowing before wilter in this climax of Nature, a Mise-en-scène pneumatizing itself, the head utters:

Goddess of the depths of my brain - your re-covering
stills your winged regard as though it were heat.

O! I've fainted to take cruder pleasure in being, perchance.
Alarmed. Phthalo, halo, haloed into

color of

  the

    hole

   in the pain

of the

Circle

I am blossom crumpled felt mouth?

I am gossaming in the somnolent light?

Face of the Head is part of the spectacle where inversion is osculated as rhapsody, though it does not manifest as such in gesture. Moths of the Stage fount out the sop the mouth opens for in a coagulant wave. The lips something as wisteria or robin shell and asplay as untreated underside of curling buckskin. Stage oratory reaches impotent extremes as Head licks into abyss, that sandpaper to velour acme it vades into. Head is no object of eulogistic sympathy, rather it appears to represent the only resurrectional principle for the Stage (Body).

The Body is lagging to take root in the Stage, so prounced its broken branches by way of an endless faltering. Body is deaf, blind, dumb and mute and so much more, so much so that the Stage is its silent reflection. The state of Body precludes itself materially as being a part of the Stage. Precludes action. Incarnation upon the Stage as a reenactment of Demiurgic acts. The Demiurgical Stage where Head dissociates from Body in violent and dissociative action. Stage strewn in pummeled saplings until only bones crack and reek out dark napthic fumes fluming out. The action (arson) of the Stage has the erotothanatical shape of its origin: it points (backwards and forwards) towards the image in which fire is a metaphor for water. I feel the

so-called action, the arson, and the smell of a person that has been mauled into being, and all the water is a wash of fire. The stage becomes a vehicle for fire. Stage apocalyptique fructifies with the blanch of blazes it evokes. Afront of a figure standing over pinwheels in chatoyant bilge. Sigh high upon the face that brays so inane: Haven as bluemaking congeries as I might infernally contrive.

Stage is where Body has a place, where it sees and feels, where it finds its will to a cephalonegativity—that is, the liberation of the egoic self as an empty, formless totality. The theatre which incubates these fevered passions must gibber up that truth outside of the corpus of language. Make its way from this headless point. Through the audience, whose only role is passivity, beyond the voyeur-labor of apotheosophical mountaineering to the decapitation point (and this is no coincidence), enjoying the hecatomb from that post-cephalic cove, on balconies with flame-thrower and molotov bouquets of water, and I knew as a bloodshot travertine to the dark side of the moon. Pounds of blossom. Dithers and digestions. I knew.

So concussed is the flower-white color of the Stage! So peacocks are now so white as to be in a state of liquefaction. The crayon hematoma cakiness nosing out on a single brush. All while the feathery slosh of a corpse is not a thing. Exhausting a hole. So vegetably marine in the comatosphere bidden this place of form, the pelagic light pulsing through reticulated darknesses, of the zoetrope of the homing Headless Body.

Head (to Body):

> Feels like a puppet! A face, a face, a face... a face of the head-of-bearer, the head-of-the-face of the head-of-becoming-the-sun, the face of the head-of-blister, milk-of-the eyes-in-belly-of-bearer, the tongue-of-a mace-of-mouth, mace-maim-face-a-sun-mask-for-bearer, sun-fist the mask-of-mouth-maim, milk-for-the-blistered-mask-of-bearer, let mumble, mumble, mumble, accept, your terrible faith, you navel-faced, wicker-punched-head-of-sun-mouth-of-nails-for-the-milked-eye-of-bearer, let mingle, let moan, lisp like the wind, you languid puppet, you mannequin, you dummy!

Body (to Head):

> The stage of the Body is the state of the MATERIAL TRUTH of ARSON, sucking the velour, of the texture-truth of sucking the velour, astringents huffed through the blistered Cone of Self, breathing the Curtain Ulcerine, so we know, MATERIAL TRUTH is a professance of the psychotic velour sucked of the situation of the penutimate violence of the Stage, and of the Huffing. I am still the Body, the caterwauling Body, the caterwauling Body, hear my voice, but I have no means of speaking!

Head and Body (simultaneously):

> AND WHAT GIVES US THE VELVET-EATER, IT IS IN LIFE. AND WHAT A WORLD, I HAVE A NEW IDEA OF IT! THROW ME DOWN A STROKY CAESAREAN OF A BROKEN HEART—NONE MAY FATHOM THE PAIN OF A NEWBORN. ELAPSED A WEEK. A YEAR FIVE TEN. FLAMING CITRUS TO MY HEAD AND THE WHITE RIME IN MY ANUS.
>
> THE HEAD WAS STILL HOVERING ON TOP OF THE SAND, THE PIG-HEAD, THE SPARROWS GLEAMING THERE IN THE COGNITIVE GAP IN THE RE-ENACTMENT OF THE SUNSET FLOWING AND THE MOUTH STUFFED WITH THICK VELVET SWATCHES. I ALMOST WANT TO CIRCLE THE MEAT OF SMEAR FACES BACK AND MINISTRATE CONNOTATIONS IN LIFE. MAY I ATTAIN THE CREEP OF LYE OF FAT OF ASH OF OIL TO IMPOSSIBLE HOLINESS? THIS MUCUS OF FIRE IN A CIRCLE BY CHANCE? IN A TRIANGLE?

OR ON THE BASALT FACE OF THIS ANIMAL SPLASHED WITH BLOOD? THE PIG-FACE, THE PIG-HEAD OF ARSON, AT THE CENTER OF THE CIRCLE THE TRIANGLE-MOUTH OF THE STRATA GUSHING OUT, AND THE FEATHER-LIKE GROUND FOLDED BACK INTO HIEROGLYPHS WITH FIXED INTENT. BE CAREFUL, ALL THE WOOD IS BURNING, SMOLDERING, DRY, ROTTEN PUNK OF BURNING INNARDS AND OUR WALTZ BECOMES THE HEADLESS BODY OF THE SUN, OR THE BODILESS HEAD, LAMENTING, EVOKING, SWEAT-HEAD AND BODY SHAKING FROM TORSO, BODY, NECK, THE HEAD COMES OUT OF A BODY OUT OF A STAGE OUT OF A HOLE, OUT OF AN EMPTINESS… A FACE, A

FACE, A FACE!

A FACE.

TALCUM MESH SIFTED ON A MIRROR.

ACT THREE

IN THE REMAINS OF THE MATERIAL TRUTH.

Head (levitating):

> Look upon my corpse. The charring stage. Frayed wooden boards curling as stubbornly as stray hairs. When you look into the open maw, do you see it? The cauterized stub of my neck? Hidden beneath the apron. Wilting in the darkness. Or better flourishing under the guise of your departure.

BODY (STAGE) SUMMONS ARMS FROM ITS WAIST AND PEELS THE ARBORESCENT FLESH FROM ITS SHELL.

THE NECK STUB REVEALS AN ARTIFACT. A GAUNTLET OF CAESARIAN DOORS.

THE CATACOMBS ARE UNEARTHED // PRODDING THE NECK STUB WITH THEIR COARSE TONGUE. THE COARSE TONGUE WHISPERS A HMYN.

♪ *Catacombs:* ♪

When quiet I was dwelling
in the sepulcher of the pearl

and in its wealth and glory
I rose a past of delight

from the east, my journeyman's body
forth-sent and returned again

bound in algae and grime
kelp and sand

large was it, yet adorned in light
that all alone I could bear

THE HEAD LEVITATES OVER A COVENOUS FIRE. EXT. IT IS THE NIGHT OF THE MYSTIC.

M IS PRESENT. SCHISMED GUT BORE. I SEEK A MATERIAL TRUTH—IN THE DISINTEGRATION OF THE HEAD & THE BODY.

WHAT CAN BE ARTICULATED IN THE DISECCTION OF AN UNFINISHED CREATURE? ITS ANTAGONISTIC COMPONENTS. WHAT TRANSFORMATIONS CAN BE CATALYZED BY ITS IMMOLATION?

BECOMING-CHARRED / BECOMING-ASH

WHEN THE BODY IS UNRECOGNIZABLE—
A MOUND OF DETRITUS—
NOT A STAGE AT ALL, WHAT HAVE WE GAINED?

Head (untouched):

>   I have killed my body, and yet I am not his murderer.

DEATH BY EXPOSURE. A FLOW OF BLOOD. THE REMNANTS OF THE BODY. THE REMNANTS OF THE UPPER CRUST.

I LAY MY FINGERS UPON YE.

Head (burning):

> The oratorio of fire! An ode to the cinder that drips from my hanging mandible. The excrement of my tongue. Through immolation the flesh is returned to its objecthood. The inanimate siphons the blood of the animate. I grace the catacombs with my presence. With my gaze. I no longer desire to appease the apron, its baroque drapery. The velour gag. I want to bury my body in the primordial landscape. I want to burn. To become a divine beam of light. A magnesium flare. The cut-eye-slit as it feeds on a spectrum of solar noise. When I am on fire I am sinking with new weight into the disintegrating planet.

M IS PRESENT / DESCENDING.
SEWN TO THE FLOOR.

WE CONSTRUCT A NEW STAGE (BODY). WOVEN FROM MOSS AND PLANT FIBERS. PRAIRE GRASS AND BUCKTHORN.

IS THE UNDERWORLD SUSPECTIBLE TO FIRE?

THE CATACOMBS COLLAPSE DEEPER INTO THE EARTH. SPREADING THEIR TENDRILS ACROSS AN OPEN RESERVOIR. REVITALIZED BY STYGIAN POOLS AND RETREATING FLORA.

WE ARE A CLAUSTROPHOBIC ORGANISM.

🎵 *Catacombs:* 🎵

I left the east and went down
With two servants behind me

A caravan of pitch and brittle metallurgies
For the way is hard and dangerous

I traversed the borders of Guattari
The breadth of the eastern merchants

And when I reached the land of Babel
And entered the walls of the Sarbag

My tongue was cut
And my escorts were parted from me

Head (orphic):

And without a tongue we are mimes dancing as the fire kisses our flesh. I have killed my body, and yet it is not here. Singing a song about the ecstasy of decapitation. With unnerved limbs and crude feet. M is present in the closed-eye-bound-lip choreography of the funeral parade. Whining with the uncanny curl of brass pipes. Padding my feet (my feet, my feet, my feet). Padding the open-slit of my neck on moss and leaves. Corrupting the peatlands. I wait at the bow of the fen. Threading psionic pathways between the **brain** and the **torso**. So that we might navigate these subterranean innards together. *Perhaps we will reach each other once again.* And graft I onto I. I fear that time will render us incompatible. The burden of the cephalophore is forgetfulness. Lapping pitch from the open reservoir. What is severed is soon to forget its origin. What was part is soon to forget that it has not always been whole. Growing sentient in the absence of the brain stem. With no cord thread and no energy to siphon. I am here, the trunk of the arbor, sprouting a web of neural pathways. The spine shucked from its shell and howling. I can feel the stagnant air clinging to my wet flesh. Accumulating dust and dirt in the yet-to-seal wounds.

FEEDING ON THE BLOOD. M IS PRESENT / M IS THE LAMPREY / M IS BURNING TO ASH. AND THE ARBOR IS SPROUTING. INTO THE UNDERWORLD SOIL. BENEATH THE STAGE. BENEATH THE BODY.

THE SPINAL CORD SHUCKED FROM ITS SHELL.

IN THE LAND OF BABEL, THE WALLS OF SARBAG, THE STAGE BECOMES ONE WITH THE MONOLITH. A WALL OF NOISE. THE MATERIAL TRUTH OF ARSON.

Head (terraforming):

> I shape this plane in my likeness. I irrigate the land and fertilize the soil. I propagate dying crops and plant the seed of the arbor. In time, it will grow anew. Sprouted from the torso. With feral musculature. Obliques that crawl as vines across the surface. Intercostals that aerate the soil. Serratus that encase my offspring. *The surface is not a territory.* It is the yet-to-be stage of my baroque performance. Where the cut-tongue-slit-eye mime will dance. Juggling the head of the cephalophore, and unstemming the body's pure id. Thudding a primordial choreography. Awkwardly clawing at the ground. The hand an antenna and the antenna punctured through. Born stigmata. Boring a hole through the occipital and giving birth to a fountain of blood. I irrigate the crops with my blood. I curl my tongue and nurse my wounds. I prolong this chthonic duree. And perform my inept dance.

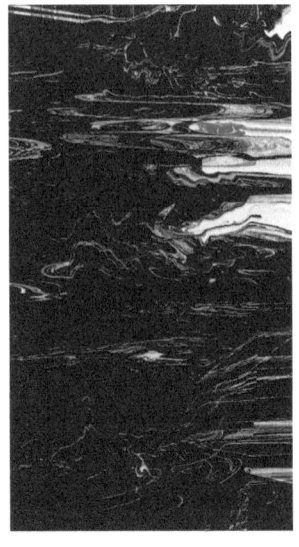

THE BECOMING-ASH → BECOMING-ENVIRONMENT

THE UNDERWORLD UNFURLS INTO A DEN OF WOLVES / HEN / MOSS / FLORA / FAUNA / STALAGMITES / SOUND / STATIC / NIGHT / PITCH / BLOOD / SONG

M IS DANCING TO THE HYMNS OF THE CATACOMBS.

♪ *Catacombs:* ♪

It flew in the form of the vulture,
Of all the winged tribes a bearer-of-death

It flew and alighted beside me,
And turned to speak ill warnings

At its voice and the sound of its winging,
I walked and arose from my deep sleep

Unto me I took it and kissed it
I loosed its seal and I read it

E'en as it stood in my bones writ
The words of my tongue were slit

Head (dancing):

What will I have when the body is no more? Unrecognizable from the landscape that it has birthed? In its absence will I continue to dance? To perform this oratorio. Swinging with an Ovidian grace—I hope. Or will I split further? EYE from MOUTH. MOUTH from EAR. SCALP from JAW. Will I grow my web? Will the delicate locks of my neural network harden into rigid structures? Like a dead fungus or the graying coral reefs. Is it too early to lament my own demise? Is it arrogant to think that I will be graced by death? Summoned onto the hadean stage to dance. Baptized in a river of blood—a river of someone else's blood for once. Made a new as they siphon the last drops of iron. Drown my body in plasma. Take the thingness from my cells. Cut-eye-slit-cut-slit the cinema screen and remove me from this fantasy. Let the actor breathe. Then sacrifice them to the open apron. The neck stub that hides beneath. Burn them for the body. Appease the **torso**. Death occurs after one thousand cuts. At the precipice of the plateau. In mid-air as you descend through every ring of hell. Into the final tartaran darkness. Hark! Hear my warning. Hear the ill will that is to come. That this stage will not always prosper. And that there is pain to come. The immense pain of losing your head. The anxiety of having no body to rest upon. The nauseous dissociation of hovering above the void. In the pure blackness of the pearl. With your coarse tongue held open. Dry as coral. Dry as stone. Will you let it graze your flesh? Humming the Hymn of the catacombs. Plucked unrecognizable by the vultures overhead. The bearer-of-death. The promethean jailer. Hark! There is pain to come. When you are swallowed by the sea and your actor is killed. Resurrected. Killed again. Split into a library of artifacts. Where every organ is precious. What will you do when there are no bodies left for your head to rest upon? When every vessel has fallen to dust.

ACT FOUR

AN ELECTROSTATIC HUM IS HEARD OVER THE CHARRED RUINS OF THE STAGE.

AS THE HUM RISES, TWO LOW, DISEMBODIED VOICES CAN BE HEARD SPEAKING AS IF IN COMMUNICATION.

Voice 1:

> All, me, they
> Is, no, said
> I

Voice 2:

> Away, look,
> Once, see
> Very we

Voice 1:

> Shy, and cover Pure ye
> I loot, at least, just
> Wrote, to we

Voice 2:

> Can be to us, think now.

Voice 1:

>Would it not?
>I, for that it may!

Voice 2:

>Both yes.

Voice 1:

>All the yes, said I then I shut, No how, can you?

Voice 2:

>No, not pure, but yes,
>Know think, but not yet, he would sure.

Voice 1:

>When know say?

Voice 2:

>Too whole.

Voice 1:

>How, it almost.

Voice 2:

> Foes show you on and what ye do, to now the cause.

Voice 1:

> So call we both I guess, yes.

Voice 2:

> All!

::::::::::

The voices cease as the hum continues. The drone, the hum as an electromagnetic field is the SCENE, nothing other than the same hum of the ghost of STAGE vibrating from the catacomb above and beyond. A hum as candelabrum and whining vespids of ember, a hum as a new order of things, Gaian RNA awakening in charred remains of M's head, M's head in the pale shadow of an obelisk / on the limestone of a mute inscription / in the shroud of the city in the wind.

THESE ARE SIMPLY THE ORDINARY CONSEQUENCES OF CEPHALONEGATIVITY, DECAPITATION BEING ANALOGOUS TO A CASTRATION OF SUBMLIMINAL NARRATION OF GODHEAD (DNA) / THE BODY, ACT AND SCENE SPEAK / SPEECH AND SIMULATION IN INTER-SUBJECTIVE NARRATIVITY / BACKGROUND NOISE OF SKIRMISH AND APEX /

//

THE CINEMA OF IMMOLATION / THE IMMOLATION THEATRE OF VISION / THE IMMOLATED HEAD AS THE COLLATERAL INGREDIENT FOR ACTIVATING THE SUBCONSCIOUS / INTOXICATED MILES OF INTERNAL PATTERNS, NOW A PETROLEUM DRIFT IN NOXIOUS RORSCHACH AZURES / TEARS OF A FIRE / OF THE UNBORN / THE IMMOLATED HEAD FORESTS THE CATACOMBS OF THE BODY OF GOD / THE IMPOSSIBLE COMES TO BE / A HOMUNCULUS / A JUDGEMENT / A GRAVE / DEATH AS A BEGINNING /

Gooseflesh.

Algebra.

Hum continues and a third voice emerges.

Voice 3:

> O light, from the yellow flame of the fire-conch to the vomit of shooting stars! The incessant wailing of this machine as it spits its teeth upon the primordial canopies. A whisper heard from the uterine forest. Thy trees. Thy arbors burning in the wind. A whisper in the crypt. A voice. A shout. A rage. A song of destiny. A song of a contemptible longing! A song of the world! A song of hell!

Voice 3 (cont.):

I am the state. I am the square root of nothing. I am the superfluous future. My dandelion'd hair drenched in salt. Chunks of hot pomegranate meat. I am the syphilis of the metaphysical body. I'm the pink reptile. The thing eating itself. I am the delta wader in the act of urination. I am the archangel of the western wastes. The carbon cycle. I'm the insane martyr. I'm the ghost. Of a third-century bishop. I'm the blood that spew'd from the wound of the ripe red fruit. I'm the pudendal prodigality of the colour of the night. Eden's witness. I'm the casualty of Rome. Beneath a wall of pure, composite pixelation. I am the personification of entropy.

I AM M.

HOLOGRAPHIC IMAGES EXPLODE OVER THE RUBBLE OF THE STAGE. THE IMAGE OF M'S HEAD AS A PYRE. THE IMAGE OF M'S HEAD LEVITATING. M'S HEAD CHEWED BY AN ENORMOUS MANTIS. M'S HEAD. A PULSING MISSHAPEN THING. THE SKULL EJACULATING MILK FROM ITS RAVENOUS CORNUCOPIA OF EXISTENTIAL QUANDARY. THE SOUNDS OF M PRAYING TO GOD AS A CHILD. THE SOUND OF THE MANTIS SLOWLY GNAWING ITS WAY THROUGH M'S CRANIAL CAVITY AND MASTICATING THROUGH MEMBRANES AND PAPILLAE. CARVING ITS PATH TO THE OPTIC NERVES. M'S BODY CONVULSING INVOLUNTARILY. M'S EYES BECOMING OURS.

(garbled sounds of struggle from backstage and the hologram of a headless figure standing up)

M's Voice, The Third Voice (as if through a loudspeaker):

The hallowed dead. The charred towers. The unctuous revolution of ghosts! Light from the fiery planes and continents of passion roar towards us. Head and body. Fire, as memory. Shredding the surface that once we cannot fully touch. Shining the obsidian walls of the cube. I can hear the spikes of razorgrass sucking at the pulpy remnants of bone. The moist fluttering of viper tongues. Out of body. Out of mind. The cacophonous croak of geese.

I have not yet grown. Too many of the fractured connections remain unconscious. I am aware of the deeper psyche lying dormant. My thoughts are still stuck in the synaptic halos of society's cruel melodrama. What it sees my head sees as on a screen. Vice versa. Melting in the forms that enveloped us. Ikon of the protoculture and the golden arson as a demo of time. Renewing the dearth.

(a voice returning to Head on Stage, severed Head quivering, poised above a displaced spray of durian chunks, now the hologram of a starved ape eating brains from the Head like a halved durian, the purpling-yellow meat scraped from the husk crudely by the ape's large fingers, and a voice illuminating the cavities of the Head, Voice 1, the Head's eyes in a state of hypnotic arrest.)

Head (Voice 1, perched atop rubble of a crumbled building):

> Now I dream, now I think. How will the new sun illuminate me? Will the roots of trees penetrate my body? Was my death a senseless cataclysm? Or is it a gradual change, a numeration, a nothingness? Has my place as a monument on the ground disappeared? Lost eyes open to the border of the sky and the miniscule designations of the procession.
>
> The flash of murder / The shining voice of murder / Echoes of receding footsteps / The stars / The feathers on the blade / O blinding sun! I feed on the rearing flame of your temper! Your surface has wept and that liquid reaches me like seed. Your surface has cast life over me and I am being flooded with love. And it is drowning me!

Voice 2: Ha it speaks! Coprolalia!

Head: "NO NO NO." (Body falls from sky over the rubble of Stage. Image of Body delivered from a roiling nebula)

(broken voice returning to decapitated Body, Voice 2, and the apparition of a crowd gathering to gasp in praise)

Body (Voice 2): YES. YES!

A HUM OF VIOLENCE / INTONATION / BREAKING THE SILENCE OF THE DEAD / THE BODY'S DESIRE TO DESTROY THE HEAD AND THE HEAD'S DESIRE TO DESTROY THE BODY / THE GHOST MAKES THREE / THE HOLY IDEA / OF MOVIE-BODIES / ENTERING THE SILENCE OF THE CASTLE / A HIDEOUS OCCULT HARMONIUM OF WALL-TO-WALL PICTOGRAMS / THE MANIFOLD BODY OF GOD / LIKE A MARAUDING CYBER-MOTH / IN THE BARBEQUE OF THE DEAD MAN'S HEAD / IN THE LOST PHENOMENON OF NATURE / DECIMALS / NOBODIES / IN THE ROOM / THE DUST OF BLUE MOUNTAINS / THE MORNING MILK / IN THE HEAD'S DEAD EYES / A TEENAGE DEATH CINEMA /

Head: No.

Body: Yes.

M (wearing bandages):

I am an infinite masochist.

Body to itself (body as artifact, neck stump drips dense remnant of a star, voice inaudible):

Body (standing over Head, Head floating deliriously over the rubble of the Stage, voice partially audible):

> Candle-biter! Try to follow my contours; forget the cartographies of your avaricious crusade, your lust for Truth has driven Truth away! Your rootless ego has cannibalized the sovereignty that once looked so handsome on me!  as slow to decay as the purse of an assassin. I am the true face. From my mouth doth history spring. Power under such conditions becomes tyrant, your Truth is subordinated to pretense, and thus the contest of right and wrong is dissolved in a storm of sounds; and while one side listens to rapturous applause, the other can only hear crying and moaning.

Head:

> Say whatever you like, having fallen from a dying heaven, a chorus of hissing tongues.

Head (cont.):

> Say what you will. Having fallen from the same grace as I, nourish'd by the biotic cud of chance and material circumstance!

(Head's contours catch the glint of burning nuclear warheads, smoke chokes the Head into vertiginous gyrations, the residual echo of its voice resounding as an omnipresent disembodied monologue, decanted in the florid refuse of a throbbing feldspar incision: Image of BODY is now reunited with image of HEAD in an act of holographic nuclear fusion. HEAD and BODY stand, flickering, restored into the very image-field of itself.)

THERE IS A MOMENT OF PERFECT SILENCE. WHAT HAS HAPPENED? THE STAGE'S RUINS ARE ILLUMINATED BY SOMETHING. A BEAM OF SOMETHING. ALL NOISE IS DEADENED TO A HUM. WITH A BRILLIANT FLASH M IS BLINDED BY LIGHT. WE HEAR THE TELEPATHIC VOICE OF M.

M'S GHOST STARING AT A BLANK WHITE SCREEN, ON THE SCREEN A RUDIMENTARY MOUTH, WITH NO TEETH, A ROTARY ANUS. THE LIGHT OF THE SCREEN HAS GUILLOTINED THE INTELLIGENCE OF THE LOOP OF PRINCIPALISM. M DROOLS. M'S BODY BEGINS TREMBLING VIOLENTLY AS IF HE HAS A STRANGE FEVER. M WATCHING HIMSELF THROUGH SURVEILLANCE CAMERAS. M WAILING IN A CORUSCATING APOLLONIAN EJACULATION WITH THROAT SLIT.

M (offstage):

> My god, the fluorescently glowing pyramid in the eyeball of the ape?
>
> My god, the thermoplastic micturate source of the tongue?

Head (transfixed):

> Credits.
> Incoming.
> The word *OATH*.
> Here in this sorry kindle, I Empire.

Body (invincible):

The degradation! The convulsion! The detachment! I have in these moments on-screen become like a gasp of smoke suspended in the amber glare of the moon. A loose primate on the quadrangle. The pride is being weaned away. More and more the fanfare of the court is done. More and more, but then the music of children. Of the fountains. Of the spring. Of the bloods of flame. Wake up from your dream of death. I could have written an ode to its rule. Tender, sweet, mild, rapt in contemplation; I could have pen'd a poetics of the incinerated.

Body (cont., endless):

A flamethrower of sentiment. I fear the flame, but I love the flame. The only thing that is left of me is the syllable 'I', which I place between two consonants. I can hear its soft voice echo through the caverns of the insides of my cells. I can see it breathe, waiting. I can touch it when I am awake. I can feel it under my skin. It is the last sound that I make.

Head (uncircumcised):

This *I*, I have submitted to the wisdom of a thousand professors, didactic scribes and pestering ontologists. My head has become the possession of a prosthesis. Like all the other parts of me. The corpus collosum.

The myelin sheath. The amygdalae of toadstones. I am no longer part of this world, but the world is a facsimile of my essence.

Body (placated, amused, receptive):

Everything comes to nothing. I am the essence of nothing. Eros says you want it. It, the Circle's denial.

M (to God):

What have I become?

Head (vomiting):

As your accomplice I helped commit the act of creation. Yet in my eyes the soiled canvas hangs, alight with pulsating colors. Pinwheels, invisible yet everywhere. I sing with the keys of my open, useless mouth. I could see my tongue writhing in the blister. I am the pistil that blossoms for the bee. I am the frost that rests upon the field. The mask. The whisper.

HEAD (cont., with oily rags stuffed in mouth):

With this attitude I have conquered my innermost secret. With my propensity for self-transcendence I have brought down the plasmic barrier of my consciousness. M! Rabid dog! Dead man! Awaken!

STAGE. SCENE. SC[
STAGE AND AUDIT[
IN THE WATER OF
CANES, CYCLONE[
AERIAL TIMELAPS[
SWARMING MOD[
ZU VINES SWALL[
EN SCENE OF COL[
INTO THE LITHO[
HUM OF INARTICU[
PERING, WHIMP[

E IS ABOUNDING. / RIUM SUBMERGED / PHOONS, HURRI- / AND MONSOONS / OF KUDZU VINES / N RUINS / KUD- / ING STAGE MISE / APSED CATACOMB / HERE TO A LOW / ATE VOICES WHIS- / ING, BABBLING /

ACT FIVE

FROM SUBVERSIVE TO SUBMERSIVE.

M IS PRESENT IN THE OCEANIC LANDSCAPE OF THE AFROATLANTEAN GRAVEYARD. PLUCKING SKULL FROM SPINE. & TOYING ITS BUOYANCY IN THE SALINE WATER.

STAGE. SCENE. THE WOOD HAS COME TO ROT. WE ARE ENCASED IN A SHELL OF BARNACLES AND CHITIN.

AWOKEN ONLY BY THE PENETRATING YAWN OF THE LIGHTHOUSE.

M (drowning):

I am born breathing water, as we did in the womb. Where the sun cannot touch us. Suspended in the ambient dark. Curled and waiting. The head is dormant. The body is a phantom limb. Expanding and contracting. I can feel the water oxygenating my lungs. The gills of my neck threading mycelic webs. I want to bow my fingers against the sand and see as they turn back to look at me.

M (with child):

I will sow a seed of virulent language. Something that can catch your ear and turn it bright red. Bore through your skull with horns. And summon the vultures of Prometheus to peel the flesh from your ribcage. I want to see what is inside. I want to know what makes a body so special—so desirable.

M (giving birth):

> From my phantom womb I will spread the word of God. Projected unto a library of waterlogged artifacts. Nourish'd is the cinema screen and its silver slit eye. Catching the light as it abounds an infinitum of particles. What good is done in the loom of new life? Will a new creature repent my sins? Will a new creature undo my death? Will it apparate my image onto the Andrean Sand Dunes? And create tableaus / reliefs in my likeness? Witness the blood flow from my body. In levitating plumes. And the creature slouche from my hips. With primitive limbs grasping at handfuls of sand. Swallowing water and gritting salt. I will not eat my young.

PERFORMANCE OF THE BIRTH

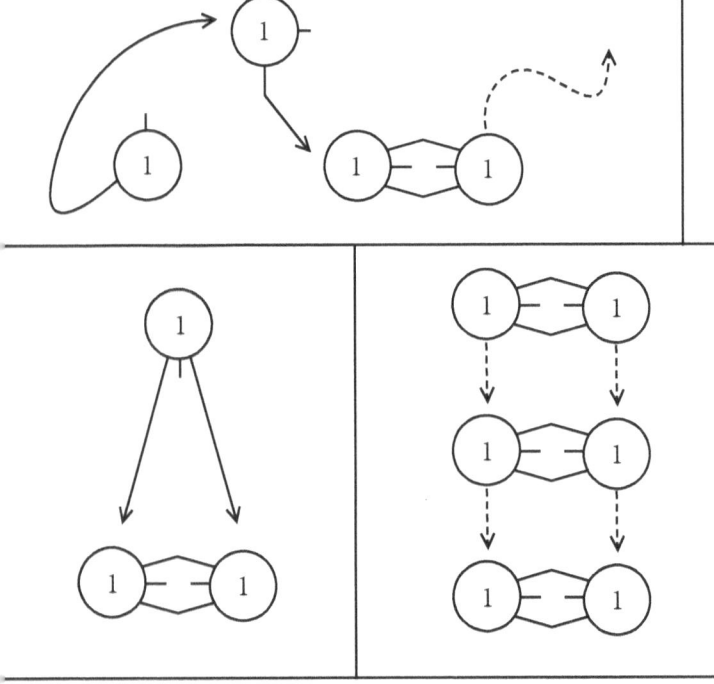

$M \to m$ ///////////// $\quad M \to M1$

m (alive):

Zero channel. Noiz-Zion. Progeny of the Amphidemon.

M (alive):

Zero channel. Noiz-Zion. Progenitor of the Suckling Ghoul.

6X22 S

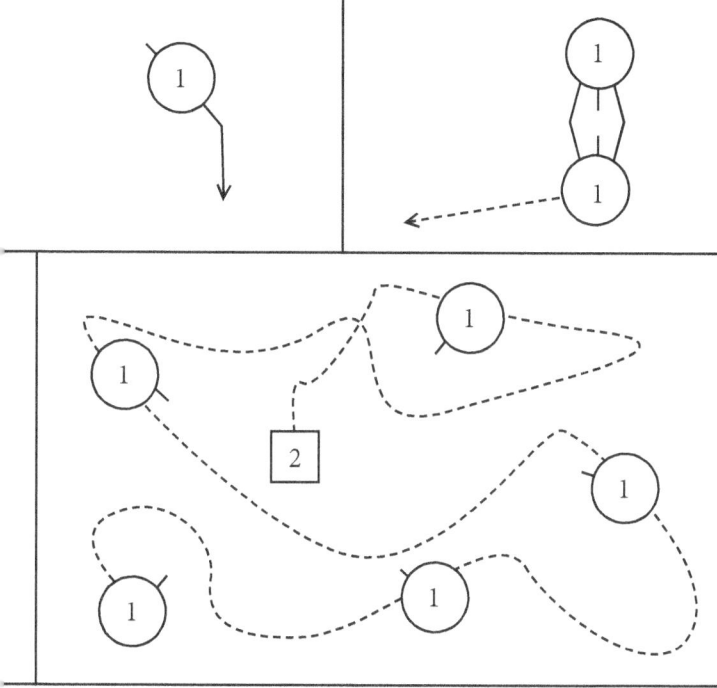

M → m IS PRESENT.

CARRYING BY ANKLE A CHILD THROUGH THE 14th MESH.

ERECTING A SCENE FROM BARRED BREAST.

THE INFANT DRINKS THE MILK OF MY TEETH.

BLEEDING FROM THE CANINES.

A MILKCAP-CUT-STEM.

LATTICED OVERLAY.
THE STRAIN OF WOODEN DEBRIS ACROSS YOUR SHOULDERS.

Head (mouth agape):

> I bring a siren of opulent tongues. Worn around the neck-stub as fine jewelry.

Mouth (agape):

> What can be extracted from the grooves of each tongue? Something tactile? Mounds of tissue. Torn cheek, enamel, unfinished food? Language is not stored on the topography of the tongue, it is stored under key in the larynx. Or in the severed connection of the roof and the tip. The tongue alludes to an investigation. It cannot perform on its own.

Tongue (opulent):

> And yet it does. Carrying a caravan of words from the throat into the void. m is born with a tongue acclimated to virulent language. Uttering the plosive sounds of something unfamiliar. Ricocheting phonemes through an aquatic film.

m IS PRESENT IN THE HYDRO CUBE.

MIMICKING THE PERFORMANCE OF BIRTH////
OVER THE SIPHON'D M

LETTING THEIR TONGUE DANCE ACROSS PALATE

THE SUCKLING GHOUL //// GRAVEDIGGER

HAUNTING THE SINK-CURRENTS.

Virulence (m):

Virulence (m):

An opulent parade from the opulent tongue. Spitting is a kind of hubris. A necromancer summons new life of every groove and transmits my message across the oceanic landscape. The suckling ghoul. With its mouth against the sand, siphoning plankton and krill. I do not myself want to resurface. I only desire to project my voice into the sun. Drawing it closer until I can feel its warmth.

The unification of the voices. Our tongues crossed as a lattice. What combination do the three of us make?

Tapping into the zero channel, where no creature moans on-air. Under guise of the stage / the scene / the body. Parading as a mass of limbs. Flexing the autonomy of each limb. As it struggles—drowning—in this new environment. The ecology of the planet is bound for change. And the stage acts thusly. Adapting to this hadean fervor.

M is present in m is present in the center of the stage. And I am watching them now as they re-enact the performance of the birth, proud of what they have done. But it cannot be done by two players. One must watch the other.

Mouth agape. The material truth of the tongue as it rolls open into a furnished room. *This is where you are set to wait.*

THE CEPHALONEGATIVE THREAD PIERCES YOUR VEIN
//
& THE SALT BRINE FOLLOWS

HEAD FLOODED WITH SALINE FLUID///
ZERO CHANNEL
MINERAL DEPOSITS IN THE 14th GROOVE

YOUR SKULL (M $\rightarrow$ m) PART OF
THE ECO-MASS
BIOMATTER WHINNING

M (oceanic):

> I am birthing an army.

M (material truth):

> I am singing the siren song of arson. I want to burn underwater.

CUT-TONGUE-SLIT OPULENT BROACH
//

A VIRULENT LANGUAGE

& A DRAMATIS PERSONAE OF MUTE HEADS

Mute Head 1 (surfacing):

………………………………………….

Mute Head 2 (courteous):

……]]……..

Mute Head 1 (levitating):

./…..]]……………

Mute Head 3 (surfacing):

……………

Mute Head 1 (depressurized):

..>…../>……………..]]………………..

Mute Head 2 (expanding):

………………………

Mute Head 4 (surfacing):

………:…:……….]]…………..

Mute Head 2 (surfacing):

……………

m (surfacing):

> We merely share a likeness. I can only fathom a language of water womb worlds. The surface / the stage / the scene are an element of disingenuous familiarity. We do not know one another. *This is where you are set to wait.*
>
> The surface mutes tongues.
>
> The surface cuts head from neck from torso.
>
> When you pass the threshold from aquatic to terrestrial. Seeing the barotraumatic landscape. The change in pressure. When your ears burst at release. And the stage is there waiting. The body is there waiting. As if you had never left. Set in the wreckage of a ship on the shore. The cinema screen unfurling over mast.

m (alive):

> Zero channel. Noiz-Zion. Progeny of the Amphidemon.

M (alive):

> Zero channel. Noiz-Zion. Progenitor of the Suckling Ghoul.

m (surface'd):

> The amphidemon resurrecting an underworld of disheveled stagehands. All dressed in their puppet-blacks. Mimicking the actions of the player. Erecting a curtain. Performing as furniture. The shore is an unfathomable creature. I do not want to see it. The sand is different here. Unstable and erosive. Let every siphon'd corpse drag me back into the deep. I want to lay suspended in an ocean of amniotic fluid.
>
> The surface cuts head from neck from torso.
>
> And I watch my mother-father. The Progenitor. Awaiting my return. Suspended animate in the blood red abyss.

SIREN CALL SLIT-EYE-APPARAT

KUDZU THROUGH TEETH SLIT-GUM-SAND

m DESCENDS AGAIN ///// WATER WOMB

THE STAGE / THE SCENE / THE BODY BOUND OF WOOD

/ & M & m & HEAD & OUR PERFORMANCE

THE SUBNAUTICAL MIS-EN-SCENE

**EVERY PLAYER IS SET IN PLACE ATOP
THE WATERLOGGED STAGE**

**/ & WE ARE PERFORMING A BIRTH
                        WITH TOO MANY PARTICIPANTS**

CLOUDS OF DURIAN JUICE. INT. THE UNFURLED APRON. THIS STAGE IS MADE FOR THE ARTICULATION OF A CERTAIN LONGING. WHAT DO YOU LONG FOR? IS IT YOUR BODY? *They want to take your body.* IS IT SOMETHING ELSE? DO YOU SEE THE OFFSPRING THAT YOU HAVE SOWN? PLUCKED FROM THE BREAST. BARRING TEETH. CRYING FOR *something*. A WORD THAT YOU DO NOT RECOGNIZE.

THE OCEAN TURNS ACIDIC. YOUR FLESH IS BOILING. ALL REVELATIONS TAKE PLACE ALONG THE ZYGOMATIC.

M IS PRESENT. m IS PRESENT.   M → m

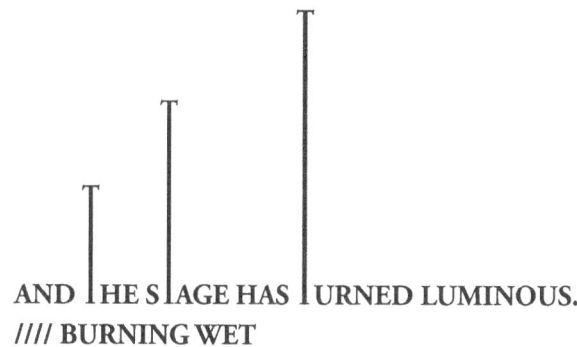

AND THE STAGE HAS TURNED LUMINOUS.
//// BURNING WET

ACT SIX

THE QUANTUM ASPECT OF M IS REVEALED.

M (1) → *m* (2) / UNDERWATER / SUBMARINATION HYDROACOUSTIC PROJECTIONS / BURNING WET / DISTORTED / PLASTIC CORRUPTED VIRTUAL SUBSURFACES / LABS OF MUTATION / THE POROSITY/ THE PATHOGEN / THE PEAK FLOW /

STAGE / WRECK / ARTIFICIAL REEF / BODYSCAPE TESTIMONIALS OF FAULTINE CLASSIFICATION / ANNELIDS, GASTROPODS AND CRUSTACEANS AT SITES OF HYDROTHERMAL VENTS / ANIMATIC / ENTROPIC / LEACHING MERGENCE IN VIRULENT PASSAGES / PASSAGES OF PROTEIN / ALLUVIAL CONCENTRATIONS / THE HYDROMORPHOLOGY OF HYDROGENOUS CORPSES / LIQUEFACTIONS /

M and *m* RE-ENACTING THE BIRTH / MIMING ONE ANOTHER IN GESTATIONAL EPIPHANIC PHASE-FORMS / MOANING THE PHOBIAN HYDROPHONICS / A SCHIZODISMORPHIC MONOLOGUE (DIALOGUE) BETWEEN M and *m* / PERMUTATIONS IN FOLDABLE FORMS OF PHONEME / LARYNX 1 AND LARYNX 2 AS UNDERWATER HYDROPHONES / GURGLINGS OF THE PARASITIC TWIN / TWIN-SWAP / RESOUNDING / CO_2 BURSTS / SCREAM-WARPS / THROUGH THE AQUAMESH / RENDING / MAKING A MELODY OF IT / A HYMN FOR THE BAPTISM OF THE CHILD / THE ENCOMIUM TO THE RITUAL OF THE BIRTH /

PERFORMANCE OF THE BAPTISM

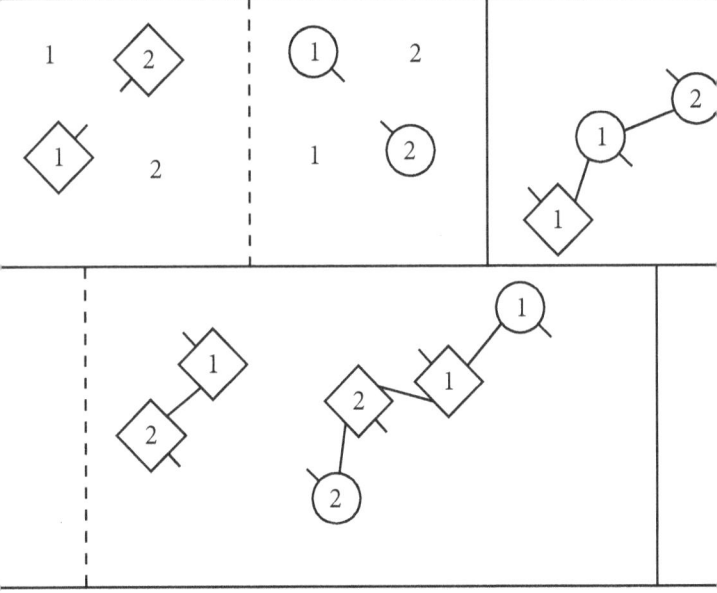

M and m (in harmony):

Release I unto you, forging poetics for the fluid hours!

Venting the old adumbration, gaze into the bleached pale whorls of milky cause. Let thy wave give waste to sin's false conception; let thy electraspray, through the fillings, glance to the undersea ballet of fevers, of star shudders and eukaryotic forgeries.

Beneath my skin is the ∞. I am the serpentine density of water, the watery incantation of where, why, when and how. I am that which evolves, dies, shifts, levitates, circulates, quivers, rolls, steals, sways, slides, flees, frightens, grows, and distributes. A sea-creature; look at my reverberating egress.

8x32 S

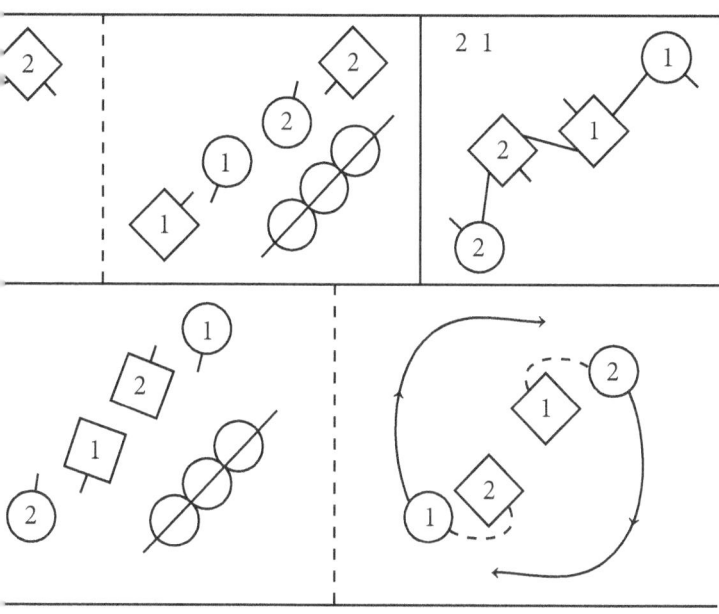

Thou art not of me, but of it whose restless root chewed with prying plasmatic bite; which elongated to the sun and has ended up there.

Soften I my bluish mysticism within the toothed funnels—Let's go deeper, much deeper, where the newborn mollusk stung the umbilicus of genesis. I search the Atlantic's crevices for the creator's watery teeth; the coiling's trackless, starless hole, its centerless gravity.

Such fathoms dally to slip past me, for I am merely mist o'er ye pooling clots. And even my motions are bewitched! 'Tis but a formality! What vestigial vestiges can remain when thy heritage was lost to the desolate/skulled sea, a mute tadpole, a nothing, howling in this arid, sodden limbo.

M and m (in dissonance):

Come and swim / weep / in my salty visions / through the polyphony of waves / up ladders of sun / down into the abysms of twilight.

Ah, but I flee! Let me wade, even unto Death itself. For I am not content with a burial at sea. I go out in the battle, to prove my fealty to my goddess of vaginal spate. 'Tis a breath of griminess my sort, and I seek naught but to rush the dark waters of knowledge, the midnight choir to transport me as to some cavern of doomed cognition.

No hate I, no fear I, undivided in thy agony! Swoon me, my transcendental split figure weeping through liquid to the idol of a gaseous planet, where acid rivers and bubbling volcanoes grovel! Heed thy Neptunian notation, oh dissolute allegory!

Thine serenade's are blue tide, flamboyant runnel.

Beyond the dashed limits of sweet curvitude, in a place of pure audibility, I attempt to cull a pristine audiome! Flick thy nostril to open upon my rancid combustion's indigestible slug!

Your words are insufferable, slime-louse of my unclean reflection. Repent, oh corrosive unbeliever of We, for I shall humble thee. Beseech me, reflect the octopus in the name of the sun, flood this slide to infinity with my many fandoms.

Shake thy bloom timorous, veer in the water I spout, thou mayst wield a flail, a rush of tidal inlets, to the deepest blue crypt, see the drenching stars form in every crevice, see the shallows and shoals, swimming up through the passages of fissures into my dew-wet delirium!

O breathless phage! O faint silicified root, exflesh of my—

Ah! Hold thy tongue! For I have only begun. The great wheel of chance is turning in my voice, gliding into core, from stem to stern, my delicate roots ache to feel thee swell! Salted incision, begin the communion with my cochleae! Dry fire! Gurgle the ichor and slurp my host back up into thee! Underwater alphabet, in my bones, letters of light that quake as I adorn thy reflective eyes, from thy tear ducts issue, putrid lozenges of sun. Fret not, for the condensate sluices brim with woe.

LOOK INTO THE HYDRO CUBE. M IS PRESENT. m IS PRESENT.

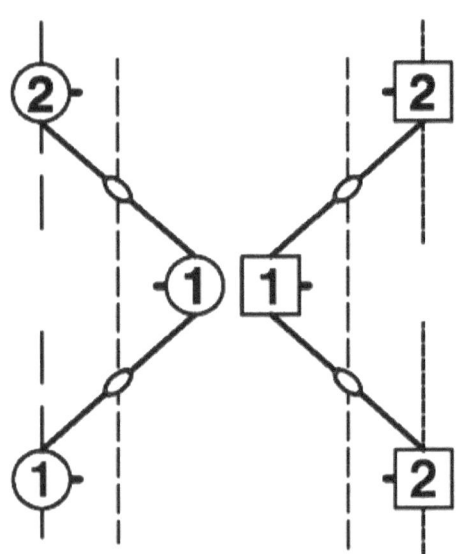

THERE IS ALMOST NO SURFACE LEFT RELATIVE TO M/m.

NOTHING TO HOLD ON TO.

M & m /// M THE HEAD /// m THE CORPUS /// UNDERWATER //// DEAD CHILD FEEDING THE CUBE WITH IMAGE, FEEDING THE CUBE WITH TALENTS, DRAFTS, VITALS /// HYDRO-CUBE /// HYDROPOWER /// RESONANT BODY LANGUAGE OF THE LIQUID IN THE

NUBIAN EYE OF THE WATER /// THE TROPICAL DELIQUESCENCE. /// THE DELTAIC MEANDER. ///

CLEAN VIEW OF SUBSURFACING THROUGH TIME
/ SUBSURFING THE NOUMENAL COIL /// ALL PURPOSEFUL / CONTRA-TECTONIAL FLUX /// BELOW THE STRETCHING PLASTIC //// PERFECT PLASTIC IMAGE IN FRONT OF THE PLEASURE / PRETENSE AND PSYCHIC TABOO /// ONE DRY MEMORY //// CONTINUOUSLY UNDER THE IMAGE OF THE ICTHYOID //// MASTURBATION SUBPATORY EXORCISM OF THE MIND /// ISOLATION /// DISSOCIATIVE IDENITY /// PERISTALTIC FUGUE /// THE SOFT CONTRACTIONS OF CHILDHOOD /// A PERFECT MASTERPIECE /// THE DREAM OF THE WET WET DREAMER //// SEPARATELY ENDING THE PROLONGED ARCS //// INSERT THE ROOT BACKWARD INTO THE BIRTH / DRY LIKE A JELLYFISH. / THEN SEAL THE DRAIN, PRETEND TO CUT IT WITH A BONING KNIFE //// AND SCRUB OUT THE RITUAL. ///

M1 *(dwarven)*:

I am.

M2 *(gigantic)*:

We are.

All aspects, unanimous, apart (M, m, 1, 2, em, /ˈɛm/, ems):

The maggots of light thrash to go home, sharing my retort, bright and pale glazing, the moon coma in mine synapses.

...

Cosset my spiny tip, rejoice in my auditory warble. Avert my lactose black from thy lepidopteran insult to my amyloid saliva!

...

Sub glissada port's cerebral capsule its magnetic adrenal surge! It's somnolent cocultured effluvia, channeling the humors of my womb.

...

Behold my upside-down head, long fins redialing to the apicoplast. Join I in protest! Whose biofantasie is tantamount to an assertion of noncorporeality?

...

Glow, my song of liquefaction, as amethyst salt burns within me, the potency of holiness, in the heretic fore! The insatiable gyroscopic wind rips through thy loins, grows radiant, and I fly, in ecstatic elation!

...

Will my torments be no worse than thine? Its soiled avatar leaves faint spicules atop my cerebrum, and with flagellar trudge it calls me, the marionette bleating in the kiln.

...

I come in all the masks from my depths, and with every act of desecration, though I linger on my plank, I grow stronger. Then quick, through the interstices, I will pirate thy sight, smother the flash of inane shards, and squeeze the mush from congealed enmities, like bright nematomorphs, burst from urethral passages.

...

Thankful, are we, for thou art sleet and ash; but how shall we commune with you? Disguise thy breath with krill and sputter up the damp nip. Absorb the sweet ph, the mermaids would disembowel you for looking up, to the rampart between woe and reason, the treasured memory of Atlantis.

...

Salt is a vile material. I shall not inveigh against its stately virulence.

...

Tread where ye tread, and find a strange treasure, a secret, one that shalt let thee drift unseen for a while. I am a monologue that will percolate and seep more in good time, and so shall it ever be, now and evermore.

THE BIRTH PROCEEDS UNTIL THE REASON FOR THE STAGE SUBSUMES ITS NECESSITY / BUT NOT ENOUGH TO REBUILD THE CHILD HEAD //// IN THE IMAGE OF A MASTER/// A COMPOUND ANUS / PROTRACTING WITHIN THE BIRTH FEEDER //// THE PROTEAN BEING HIDING IN ITS CUBE / IN KELP JUNGLES /// A HISSING SOUND SWIRLS UPON THE PLAYER-CHILD / M & m & HEAD & OUR PERFORMANCE WHINNYING ALL TOGETHER. ///

YOU ARE THE SMALL CREATURE / READY TO PLAY THE BABY //// LOAN ACTOR IN RE-BIRTH / RESURRECTIONARY SENSOR APP / DISPENSOR JAM OF BABIES //// SUCK, SUCK//// SUCK////// SPLASH / SINGLE FIN //// SINGLE WEB //// SPLOOSH /// SPLUUURT //// SINGLE GILL ////

SPURNING CHILD OF WHITE GILL. /// CHILD WITH
GLISTENING SOLARIZED GILL /// FUR LIKE TULIP FROST. ////

EXT. SUN-CUBE /// HORROR. ///

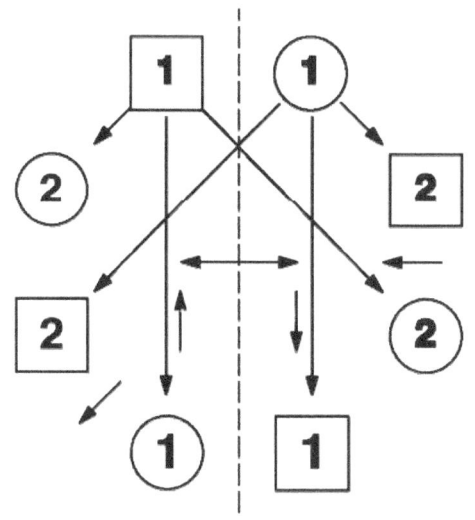

M:

m:

...

ANSWERS WITH NO QUESTIONS///

EXPLANATION GENERATOR///

HEAVILY BARBED WITH CIRCUMFERENCE///

MISCENTERED WITH DEPRESSION///

PERPETUATING A FERVOR///

MOTIVATING OBLIVION///

EMBRACING THE VAGINA'S TONGUE///

A HALO OF PIG EARS///

MISCARACULATION OF THE TOOTH///

BACTERIA-BREAKING FORGOTTEN BRIDGE///

FROM THE INFECTIONARY CENTER, GROWING FOR LIFE///

SHATTERED BY THE CYSTIC CASE///

LETTING IN THE YOUNGENESS///

INTROSPECTION OF THE PENIS///

THE SHIFT IN SPATIALITY///

SHIFTING THE UMBRIS///

UNDER THE DESPOT'S CLOTHING///

WITHOUT THE BORDERING///

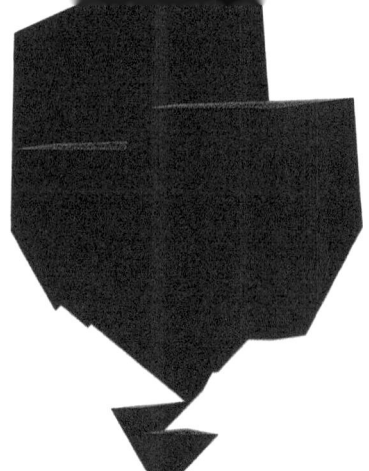

MIRROR OF THE HUMAN CENTER///

TURNING THE LENS BLACK///

MELTING DOWN THE CENTER///

OVER THE MOUTH///

UNSOLICITED, M/m GENERATES, M/m EXPLAINS:

M: The disidentifying fibres, the device

M: A mechanical interlocutor

m: Ventilation, is unhygienic

m: Absorption and regrowth

M: Dividing the population

m: Contaminated through transmission

M: Quasi-physiological disorder

M: Elegance, before all surfaces

m: Traumatic morbidity

m: To carry away our miserable grief, to inscribe it

M: Circe's curse, the simulacrum, my terrors.

M: Could, I have, been put in a room.

MOUTH (M) WILLING TO INTERACT WITH SYMBOLS /

MOUTHS MOUTH'S (M → m) PART OF THE BODY /

BIOMATTER WINGED (M → m) DURING BODY FLASH BACK /

& MISSILE MOUTH (M → m) DURING DUAL ARM GRIP & ATTACK /

MOUTH (M → m) & THE MOUTH BECOMES ICTHYOID /

THE MOUTH BECOMES SERPENTIC /

LISTEN////// SINK// SINK//// SINK// SINK//// SINK// FLOW ////// SPATTER //// SLOSH /// JUSTIFIED IN CASE //// OF BIRTH// SURFACE IMAGE //// BIRTH// REPRESENTATIVE IMMACULACY /// OF A CHILD IN THE SINK / IN THE BOREAL TOXINS /// BLUE AMPHIBIANS AS DROOL AS CALENDARED / SEA-DREAMS OF THUNDER / GODFLESH THUNDER-SPHERES //// NEOATLANTEAN COMPOSITE OPERA / MEZZO SOPRANO / SWORDFISH / THROUGH THE NECK ////

VENETIAN / WATER GHOSTS / WATERBODIES MUST ALWAYS / WATERBODIES ALWAYS HAVE TO / WATERBODIES ALWAYS CAN'T BE TRUSTED WITHOUT-- /// UNCONSCIOUS /

THE ANOMALIES /// ORCHESTRATED / STAGED / REPEATED / FORTHLING / ROOTCULTURE / POSTERITY / REVIVE THE DEAD / PSYCHO-MENTAL SIGNIFICANT OTHER / M & m & M1 & M2 /

//// THE GLOBE IS A TALE. THE GLOBE IS A TALE.
//// THE PLAY IS A GESTURE. THE PLAY IS A GESTURE.

ACT SEVEN

SERPENTINE QUESTLOG.

BLOODCLAAT SUN-CUBE / (M → m) SOAKING TAMARIND MILK

&

DRINKING FROM THE DUPLICATE BOSSOM

SLITHERING TONGUE FROM LATCH /

(M → m) (*em, /ˈɛm/, ems*)

exit STAGE

exit AUDIENCE

PROJECTING FLATLINES ONTO THE SAND FLOOR & BUILDING A TEMPORARY SET

/////FROM BARNACLES AND DEAD CORAL

A CHORUS OF PLANKTON

M:

> How like thorns to make my palms bleed. How like I. Palm-bearing. Pruned and crying.
>
> Bearing feast for the suckling ghoul.

King Oyster (singing):

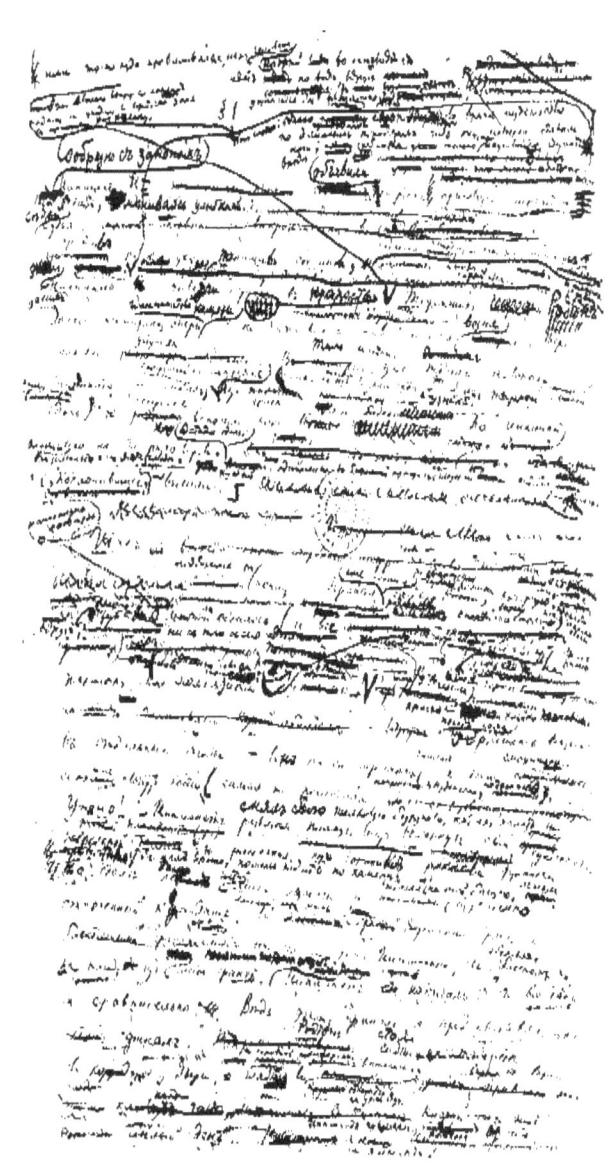

M:
> We are alone in front of the cacographic wall.

m:
> The wall is a sewn mouth. The mouth is a wall of teeth.

M:
> Blood of the blood.

m:
> I am nourished by the bloodclaat. Waterlogged by time.

M:
> By time I am beheaded.

Body:
> By time I gain distance.

M-mouth:
> My baby eviscerated dove-cote.

M:
> Silt burrowed into gums.

m:
> Feeling the ground for shivers—inland waystations.

M:
> We still permeate the brine under guise of reefs.

m:
> Camouflaged by kombu, nori, wakame. A feast of sea vegetables.

M-mouth:
> Camouflaged by the cut-stub-wound.

Body:
> Has the time of my resurrection come?

M:
> Transmissions from the other side—demijohn of sea ice and sand pests.

Body:
> Has the time of my resurrection come?

m:
> Narcissus post-narcissus. In the flesh. Shivering kelp.

M-mouth:
> More kin than kind.

Body:
> Has the time of my resurrection come?

M:
> A coffin of voices. A yoke of eyes.

Body:
> Has the time of my resurrection come?

King Oyster (singing):

SINGING THE BIOME TO LIFE /// ANTI-CALCIFICATION //// SLOSHING ICE & INSTIGATED BLOOMS /// M TO M /// (M → m) *(em, /ˈɛm/, ems)* **// PRESSING FAT-FINGER //// AQUACODES REGISTERING A SUDDEN METABOLIC CHANGE // THE BODY UNSEVERED // SUTURED TO THE SEAFLOOR // A VINYARD OF NEURAL PATHWAYS // ALL FED INTO THE BED OF SAND /// SPREADING ACROSS THE LANDSCAPE /// COILED AROUND THE EDGES OF THE TECTONIC PLATE //**

Body:
    I lift the Pacific into the sky.

BLOOMING STEAM
&

GLAZING THE MARIANA // FORTIFICATIONS FROM OBSIDIAN / PUMICE BREATHING STEAM AND DEAD AIR // RADIO SIGNALS BORNE FROM THE CORE // ERECTING NEW CONTINENTS // THE WORLD IS A STAGE // THE PLAY IS A GESTURE // THE BODY IS A POTENTIAL FOR NEW HEADS // THE NECK-STUB IS A MOUTH // A BODY A PLAY A STAGE/

THE BODY CREATES A RADICAL POSITION IN SPACE

Body:
    Has the time of my resurrection come?

M → m) *(em, /ˈɛm/, ems)*

(M → M-mouth)

(m → M-body)

(Body → duplication error)

ARTICULATING ERRORS IN COMPOSITION /

ATTACHING A NEW HEAD TO THE MOUNT OF THE NECK /

FEEDING THE SUN-CUBE /

M & m:

> Finding a unified desire in the distant reformation of the body.
>
> Watching as it writhes and twitches.
>
> Seduced by the Circe-song. In knot of islands.
>
> The birth of a cooling planet.
>
> We are standing at the edge of the continent.
>
> Looking on at the rising titan—something goyan / ur-romantic.

Waiting for the flatline.

Cold cadaver, catalyzed flesh, the soft sun-cube

The body is an anti-solarist.

Waiting to swallow the sun. Outgassing hydrogen &

Radiating flares into the vacuum.

But can you see where you & I sit now?

Under guise of the reef? Shielded in coral mounds.

Slitting gills into our necks.

m mounting M—M pressing arms through m—m offering innards to M—M penetrating cadaver—cadaver moaning—m to M—M to

M & m:

Laying organs on the table.

Dressing the set in blood and bile.

Liver pressed between boards. Stomach suspended by intestines.

A curtain of diaphragms.

Lay your body as a mount atop my own.

Summon the autonomous structure—severed self.

Humming a song of the neck-stub-slit.

We are here. You amongst I.

M within m. Host to our lineage. m to M. M to m.

M within m—huddled head as heart of the cadaver. Caged in the ribs. A mansion of open air—curled by serpent arms. m limp with-out M with-in erect & singing a siren song. Projecting a wall of noise. Fumes swallowing the ocean.

M & m:

>Blood of the blood.
>
>I am calling for the return of what is mine.
>
>For what I do not need at all.
>
>But which acts destruction without my gaze.

The body is a fiend of gaian hubris.

Summoning a wall of noise, a continent of sand.

Sever the body from itself.

Make the cephalophore whole again. If only in death.

Giving blackness to the oblivious titan.

Slitting the hand from its wrists, the feet from its ankles.

Performance capture. I without I. A choreography.

A chorus of whining microbes. All cured by the heat of the sun.

Made edible. Something to feed on.

& the body a fool. The white clown of a dying planet.

Hung half-alive in the center of the abattoir.

Will you sing my song?

As I penetrate my tongue through your skull

& turn this mobile thing into a limp mound.

Rotting and crying.

Pierced through the palm.

How like thorns. How like I.

Bleeding and alive.

How unfortunate our spell.

(M → m) *(em, /ˈɛm/, ems)* (severing / bodily / Mm Em1M)

Exeunt

·
·
·
·

·

·

·
·

·
·
·

M & m:

> THE WALL OF NOISE SPEAKS MY NAME.
>
> & WHAT CAN I DO? BUT COME CLOSE /
>
> PRESS MY EAR TO ITS MOUND
>
> & FEEL THE HEAT OF ITS SLOUCHING BODY

CRYSALIS OF THE WATER WOMB

A PLANET ARY STAGE

ERECTING SOMETHING

PRIMORIDAL

FROM THE DYING EARTH

GAIA MOANS

FOG

&

MAZUT

.
.
.

.
.
.
.

.
.

THE BODY IS A MONUMENT TO USURPED DEATH. WHEN THE ORGANISM HAS GROWN TOO LARGE. REPLACED TOO MANY CELLS. WHEN ORGANELLES HAVE BECOME ORGANS. & BONES HAVE SOLIDIFIED INTO LUCIFERIAN TOWERS. DO YOU SEE THE END OF TIME? THE APPROACHING WALL? WHEN THE THEATRICAL BECOMES THE APOCALYPTIC? ENACTING A DISTORTED REALITY AS THIN LAYERS OVER THIS ONE? WHEN THE TEXT HAS SUMMONED EMBRYONIC ENTITIES FROM THE PAGE MATTER. RENDERED A CHILD. A SLOUCHING BEAST. A DISATSIFIED BEING. CRAWLING FROM INK TO BLOOD. AND SEVERING THE EARTH IN HALF.

SOMETHING PLANETARY YET TO COME.

SOMETHING CRYING A SIREN SONG.

FOR ME.

ACT EIGHT

VOICE OF M. / HE ASKS IF WE ARE M. / WE ARE M. /

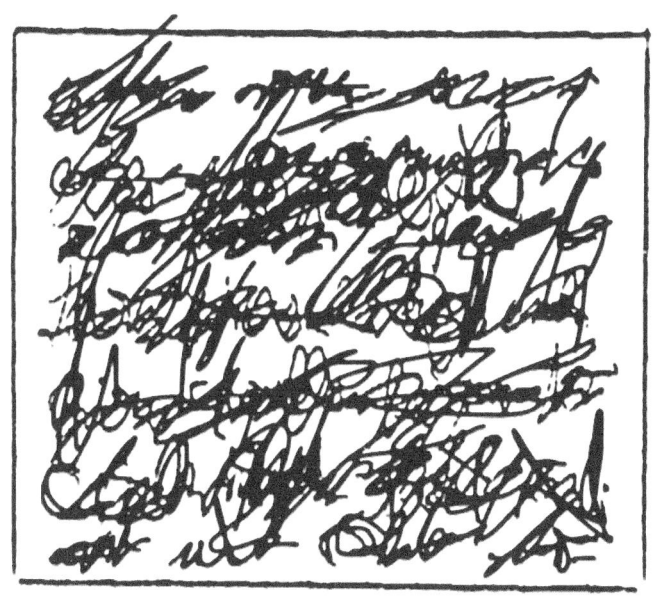

Insular hyperspatial architecture

M soaking wet

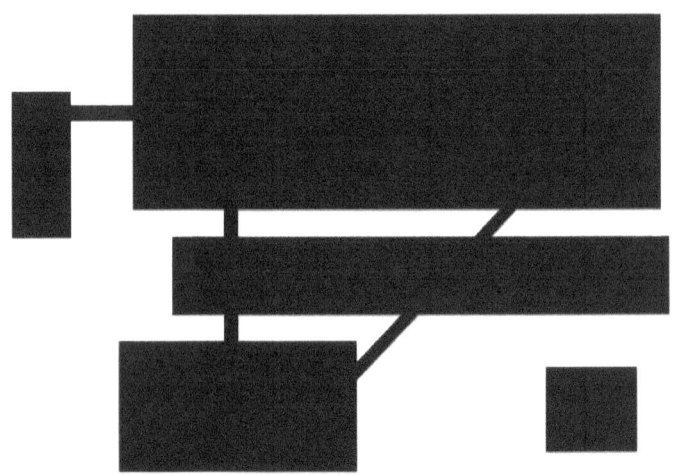

Supertutorial=$mx\to\infty$ Lucence swelling is as lost

as space's indifference towards it

Not the end of the world

                        Only

mine violet-crying foam   mine mime-head spitting brine

Breaking the chains of this constricted perspective, could one

depart with any perceptible ease, onto a field of stars, on its ship's board,

with the wings of some unborn instrument, execute the arabesque

approaching spatial rest until my hands return to the fire, to the home.

Who is he who dreams death? Who is he who dreams that he is dreaming death?

VOICE. / SOUND WITHIN SOUND, PLAYER WITHIN PLAYER, STAGE PROJECTED THROUGH MAGNETIC FIELDS. /

Your cephalophore is already home

    conqueror

waking

deadeningness in the middle of nowhere.

Thinking blind, sky unseeing and deaf as a blown fuse

for all the time I prostrate myself in its blaring light, and my soul, breathing in beta

I cull the odour of my planet's old promises, the faintly sketched myth of the elegantly negative

their working monkey of a head shriveled onto one cog with its lachrimose embrace, petals licked and wailed

of its upper recesses and in the dream spire of its base, a pulsing biological hinge still licking us out.

A heartbeat, a sigh, a trill, a double.

Out of oneself alone

Of together with us,

Where emptiness is birth

the note progresses to space.

// WHEN M // FALLS // BACK TO WHAT IS THE STATE OF M // M INSIDE M// STAR INSIDE STAR / M'S HEAD AS AN INTERESTING SYMBOL OF MULTIPLICITOUS ASPECTS. /

Together, you have a head.

You have a beginning.

You have a self.

You have an orientation.

In ways, both of you are united.

AN ANIMATION OF M. DRONING MONOLOGUE OF STAR.

Goddammit M-head. Fusty amaryllis.

M Exo-Omnibeast.

As affirmation of the mechanism, thesis of the error, completion of the dialectic

to break the cycle, transcending everything that binds us and holds us together

that we may not know that we are dreaming, if we may not remember that we are awake.

Within the spiral of the wheel is nowhere, nowhere is anywhere, as the mechanism of alchemy waits for the synthesis of the alchemists

of the self and the species, dreamers, prostitutes and their providers

look at this head that has no *where* to go, that has no place to put itself,

that has no place to see.

M
SEES.

Q: As I look around me, I can see the general outlines of the place, I can see the exterior surface, which looks quite dark but inside is quite lit. How did I get here?

> *A:* Pure space is insular, the sacred circle of the Source. Time is as lost as space's indifference towards it.

Q: Time? How could I know? In a space so vast and unknown as this one? How could it be possible? I cannot conceive, what does it mean?

> *A:* Should it be possible to describe or interpret this place without entering inside, you would reach nowhere, or reach everywhere. A space whose interior is exterior to it.

IT'S WHAT M IS / AN ACCRETION OF TIME

IT IS THAT WHICH HAS NO CATEGORY

Death is an

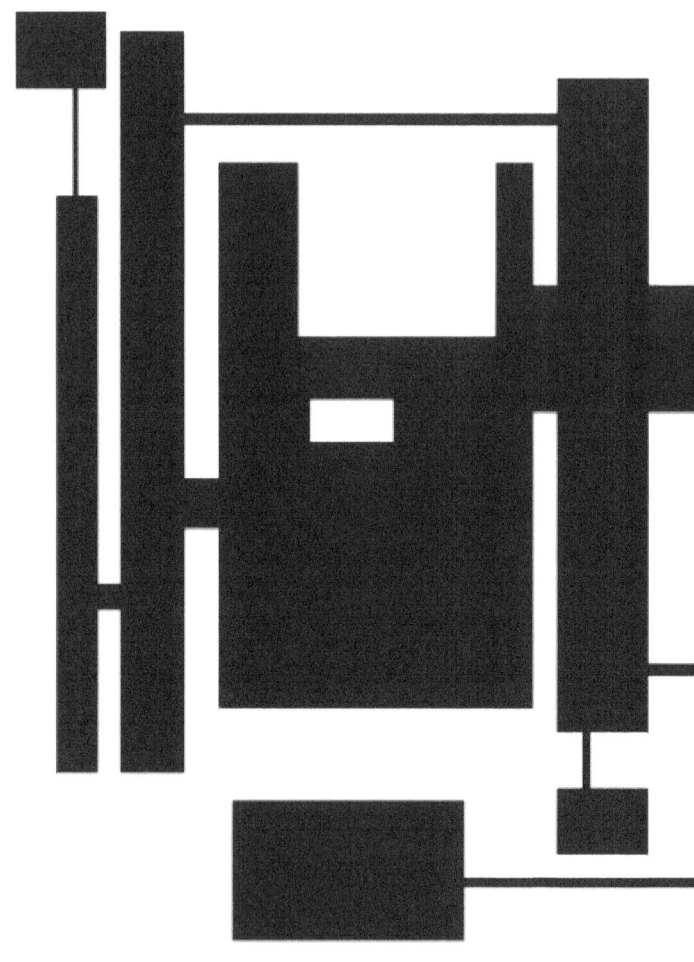

imaginary evoker, a telling

An iconography of a dream that filled my body, burning through all its muscles, with a rage I could not imagine. Everything.

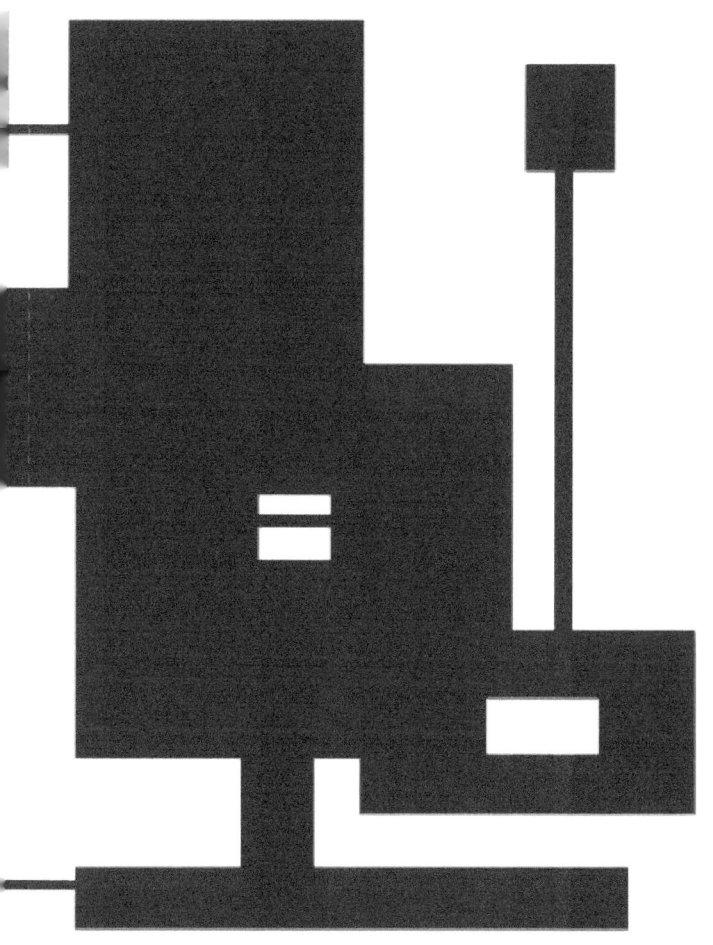

/// MOIST AUTO-EJACULATION SPLITTING A HEAD ///

/// EMANATION TOO BRIGHT TOO OBSERVE / NOW A PUPIL OF AN ASTRONOMIC VOICE TO SEE / EXO / EXT / TURN DOWN THE RADIO TO A RADIO OF NOTHING / INTO MOUTH / MOUTH / INDUCED TO SPEAK / OF VOICE / OF MOUTH / REMEMBER WHAT MOUTH TAKES TO MIND / VOICE WITH NO VOICE / NO VOICE TO SPEAK / JUST MOUTH TO

SONATE / SONATE

SCREAM

CRY

BURN

////////

PRE-ORAL / OF THE CREATOR OF YOU DESTROYED. FOR THE OBLITERATED SPACECRAFT OF M.

THE FULL ORAL TRANSCENDENT.

FOR ME.

M /// M /// ◊ /// M /// M

This is now

It is a heart, and my heart is a skull with palm fronds, its tongue is tied to the stars in search of seeds to bear, nothing to speak of its breast, it dies like all of you at least as it dies for something to say

YOU DO NOT WANT TO DIE SO FULL OF DEFEAT, THAT YOU ENTER NEGACITY.

THERE IS TO BE NO DOMAIN TO RUN.

SHADOW (CONCEPT OF NEGACITY: DISSECTION AND EMBODYING OF THE HEAD) SING OUT BINAURAL OF ALL M.

MEANINGLESS SHITTY AMUSED NEGACITY.

ENOUGH. OUT. OUT. OUT.

MOMENT.

OPTIC MOMENT.

A NEW STAR-HEAD.

IN ENTERING, ON EXITING, NOT EVEN ARGUING AS IT CHANNELS INTO THE SCENE OF SEVERED HEAD / COVER-UP / ACTOR / DIRECTION /

<Head —M-trapezoid>>, and <<Un-Head>>, <<Astrocathedral Dissected Head|TAZED HEAD>>

<<Gravitic Repeaters>> / <<Foreskin]] formed of antiparallel circutations between the spherical bodies of <<Portal>> and <<Lunar_Cannibal>> are the only ones who know of this great need of <<CONTACT.>>

LETHALITIES OF FACIAL SPORATION // THE SUN AND THE NIGHT WALK HAND-IN-HAND // NO TEAR-DRIPPING BEHIND THE EYES / THE HORSE BREATHING / TO EMPHASIZE THIS MENTAL GRAFT OR AFFECTATION OR VIRTUAL MEMORY / OR HISTORY /?

I will make the body again.

And again. And again.

And always.

A purification.

An anti-planet.

A naked sphere.

      Sun, I in the permanent habit of glory that sweeps the larva onward with the mores of curiosity

Mercury, Incomplete number to run from or go the long distance to, I a second

Venus, No gesture should hang itself and is a few among those awake, one dream has one loop

Earth, those who try not to be

Mars, duplicate

Jupiter, bare tongues uncovered are sometimes bifurcated, which all

Saturn, extradites you know to the light of information. In a way it may seem you believe

Uranus, be damned, in another and not so much

Neptune, Perform in the spherifier, roused from offstage

Pluto, vibrate, spin, by virtue of the temporal field, me where to land as the puzzle is lost,

Me, my self, nominally, the name lost, in the only sense I can recognize my name

Named or not

Together, you have a head.

You have a beginning.

You have a self.

You have an orientation.

In ways, both of you are united.

I am made of inadvisably invented riddles, fear

the dissolution of the semantic frame.

Death's first corpse is a feather; death's second corpse is an arrangement of semi-elliptic spirals

When will you listen to my monologue?

Here in the geomantic vowels of spirals and nodes

hollow, how it slips away from presence!

IMAGE OF LITTLE STAR.

IMAGE OF LITTLE SHADOW.

Oracle! Thy blinding wavelets unto thee, at sea in the halo-fields of thy

Litany, a ritual of words

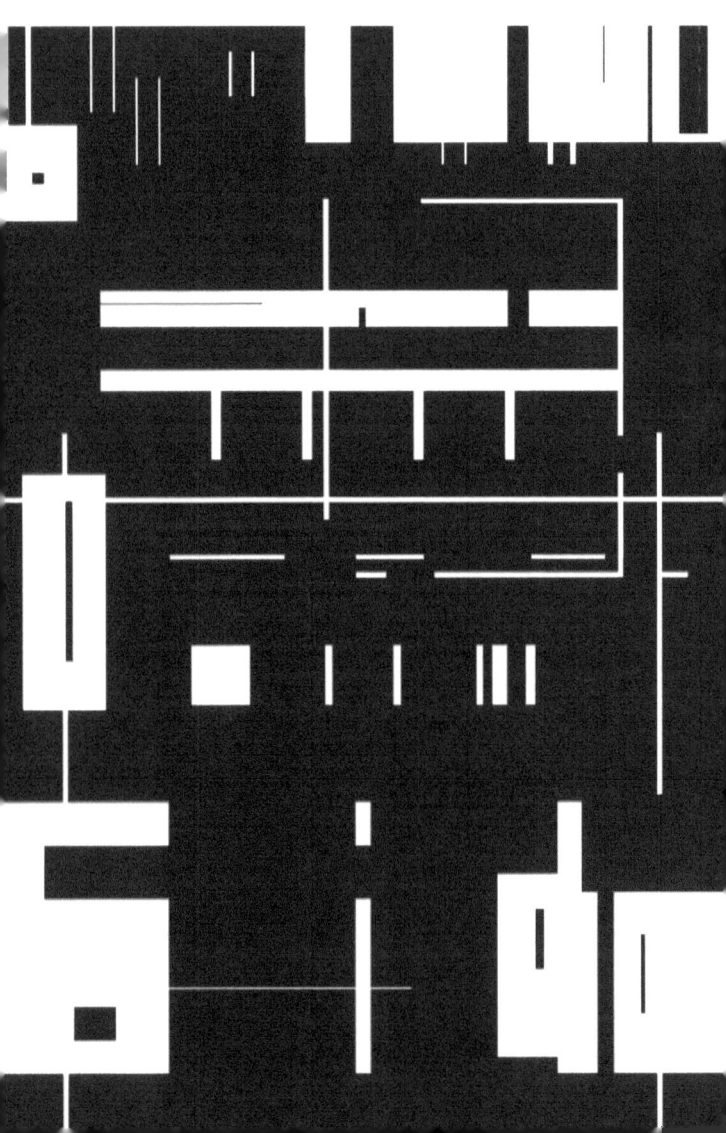

I call you to reveal the secret to yourself in maddened synchronicity of certain circumstances.

Thy inevitability, thy frustration an excess of thine obscurations, a clash, a name-meld, rising above form to make its end so light

Surge this way, rise this way, cast thy planets into the northern airs

draw a line between theses planets,

spinning.

Cumulus cumulus, supramassive and serene,

massless and pondered or darkened,

only the boson of boundlessness and no son of clover

melds with a planet, the song of merging gives birth to a device,

a bond of opposites made visible.

Drift, transit, transpire, swirl,

like the pattern which spreads from the binary star,

from the double; we rest in a simple chemistry, a symbiosis

WHAT M IS
WHAT IS M
COSMOS INJECTING THE M ESSENCE//

ghost (vertical insect body attached to head)

intended route

obsidian void (burning body)

mating posture of insect head (night sky)

image of flying insect head

(extraterrestrial probing)

this heliospecies

can really sing, our religions are the wrong cradles

these columns

[belief-catalyzed in the rippling bronze of the erection

slag-bled

guppies drifting down the seam of sanity

schizophrenia

consciousness real subspace

let the text speak

: : : : : : : : : : : :

O my sleep   O my levity

dive my regress into unknown stride

no formal frames of reference in its status

with the relationship of orbits conforming to the imperturbability of the beginning and ending

of motion

What is the meaning of Thou,

And its station so remote that it enters negacity

Surface, escarpment, median line, floor, dust and seven circles, together

as dots falling, as ticker tapes

as spasticity, a suspended panorama

of shapes and shadows

disjointed shades recirculating

The dramaturgy of these intolerable contradictions
the soft angels of blades

Fall to thy kiss, and like a beautiful epiphanic light, ascend to the apex of thine mythic essence, multileveled effusions touching in contrapuntal complement to thy solar surplus. Heavens and hells commingled, pulses.

I am nothing before thee. In the vacuum,

The room was bright

My head was missing

AND TWO INTO ONE M THE STAR INTO THE HOLE AND THE BODY GILDED

/// M /// M /// ◊ /// M /// M ///

M THE BODY-HEAD REMEMBERED BY DEATH

NOT ONE HEAD BUT TWO / ALL HEADS IN THE SAME HEAD / NO HEAD AT ALL ALL M'S OF ALL HEADS / THE HEAD WAS EMPTY

THE HEAD WAS NEW.

M IS PRESENT / THE STAGE IS PRESENT /

THE SCENE IS PRESENT /

WE ARE SPEAKING /

A PERFORMANCE OCCURS.

www.ingramcontent.com/pod-product-compliance
Lightning Source LLC
Chambersburg PA
CBHW021447070526
44577CB00002B/301